OUR GALAXY AND BEYOND

URANUS

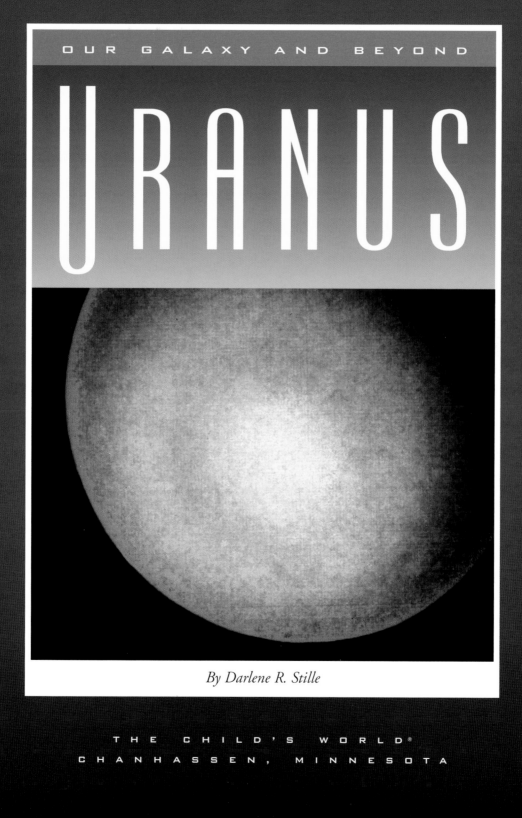

By Darlene R. Stille

THE CHILD'S WORLD®
CHANHASSEN, MINNESOTA

The Child's World

Published in the United States of America by The Child's World®
P.O. Box 326, Chanhassen, MN 55317-0326
800-599-READ
www.childsworld.com

Content Adviser:
Michelle Nichols,
Lead Educator for
Informal Programs,
Adler Planetarium
& Astronomy
Museum, Chicago,
Illinois

Photo Credits: Cover: NASA/JPL/Caltech; Bettmann/Corbis: 4, 5; Corbis: 6, 15 (James A. Sugar), 16 (Roy Morsch), 17, 23; Heidi Hammel, Massachusetts Institute of Technology/NASA/JPL/Caltech: 10, 13; NASA/JPL/Caltech: 7, 8, 9, 11 (Kenneth Seidelmann, U. S. Naval Observatory), 14, 18, 19, 26, 27, 31; NASA/Roger Ressmeyer/Corbis: 20, 22, 25.

The Child's World®: Mary Berendes, Publishing Director
Editorial Directions, Inc.: E. Russell Primm, Editorial Director; Dana Rau, Line Editor; Elizabeth K. Martin, Assistant Editor; Olivia Nellums, Editorial Assistant; Susan Hindman, Copy Editor; Susan Ashley, Proofreader; Kevin Cunningham, Peter Garnham, Chris Simms, Fact Checkers; Tim Griffin/IndexServ, Indexer; Cian Loughlin O'Day, Photo Researcher; Linda S. Koutris, Photo Selector

Library of Congress Cataloging-in-Publication Data
Stille, Darlene R.
  Uranus / by Darlene Stille.
    p. cm. — (Our galaxy and beyond)
Summary: Introduces the planet Uranus, exploring its atmosphere, composition, and other characteristics and looking particularly at how humans learned about the seventh planet from the sun. Includes bibliographical references and index.
  ISBN 1-59296-056-1 (lib. bdg. : alk. paper)
  1. Uranus (Planet)—Juvenile literature. [1. Uranus (Planet)] I. Title. II. Series.
  QB681.S794 2004
  523.47—dc21   2003006337

TABLE OF CONTENTS

CHAPTER ONE

DISCOVERING URANUS

For many years, **astronomers** did not know that Uranus was a planet. They saw a dot of light in the sky and thought it was a star. That idea was changed by British astronomer William Herschel. At first, Herschel thought Uranus was a **comet** when he saw it in the night sky. He watched its movements and figured out how it orbits, or goes around, the Sun. Then, in 1781, he decided it was a planet. All the planets, except Earth and Uranus, were named after Roman gods and goddesses. Uranus was named after a Greek god—the god of the heavens.

Uranus is a big planet. It has a diameter of 31,765 miles (51,118 kilometers).

William Herschel first thought Uranus was a comet, but he later decided it was a planet.

Uranus was the name for the Greek god of the heavens.

A planet's diameter is the length of a straight line going through its center, from one side to the other. Uranus's diameter is more than four times greater than Earth's diameter, which is 7,926 miles (12,756 km). Even though it is so big, Uranus is hard to see from Earth because it is so far away. Uranus is the seventh planet from the Sun. Its average distance from the Sun is almost 1.8 billion miles (2.9 billion km).

Sometimes it is closer and sometimes it is farther away because it travels around the Sun in an oval-shaped orbit.

Astronomers study Uranus with **telescopes** on Earth. They also use telescopes on spacecraft in orbit around Earth. But most of what we know about Uranus came from a visit by a spacecraft named *Voyager 2.* This little spacecraft flew past Uranus in 1986. *Voyager 2* carried no people, but it had cameras that took thousands of pictures. Its instruments made measurements of Uranus. *Voyager 2* sent the pictures and measurements back to Earth. Astronomers learned much about Uranus from the information that *Voyager 2* sent them.

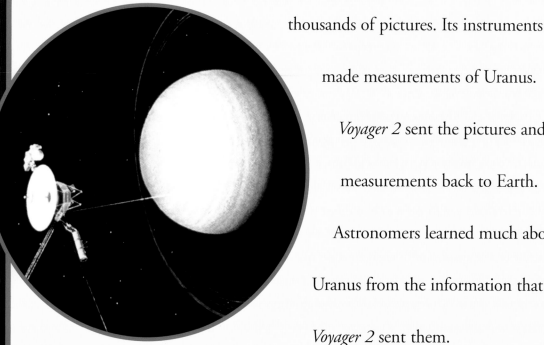

Voyager 2 flew past Uranus in 1986.

CHAPTER TWO

URANUS'S ATMOSPHERE

As *Voyager 2* flew past Uranus, it took the first close-up pictures

of the planet. At first, Uranus looked like a smooth, blue-green ball.

Scientists used computers to make the pictures sharper. They studied

measurements from *Voyager 2*. They found that Uranus looks so

At first, scientists thought Uranus resembled a smooth, blue-green ball.

smooth because it is covered with a haze of smog, which is a thick,

smoky fog. This is the same kind of smog made by automobiles

on Earth!

Of course, there are no cars on Uranus to make it smoggy. The

haze is caused by a gas called ethane in Uranus's atmosphere. An

atmosphere is the layer of gases that surrounds a planet. Most of

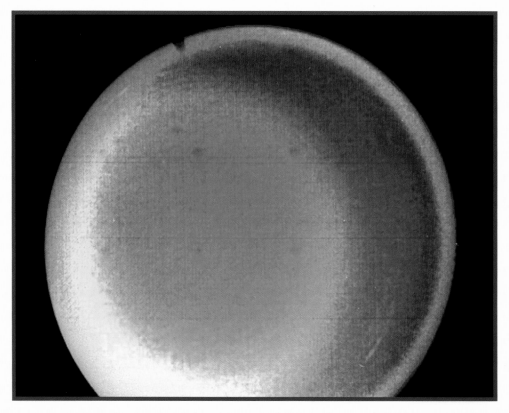

Scientists used this photo to study Uranus's atmosphere.

Uranus's atmosphere is hydrogen gas. Hydrogen makes up 83 percent of the atmosphere, and helium makes up 15 percent. The rest of the atmosphere is methane and ethane gases.

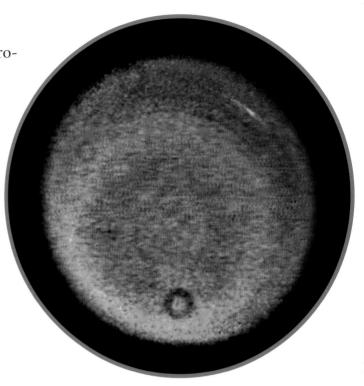

Voyager 2 *photographed a cloud streak on Uranus, shown here in light pink in the upper right portion of the planet.*

Uranus has thick clouds underneath its layer of smog. The clouds are made of methane, which makes the clouds look blue. Strong winds in the atmosphere blow them around the planet. The clouds form a striped pattern. These striped clouds are difficult to see through the smog.

The Hubble Space Telescope saw very bright clouds in the atmo-

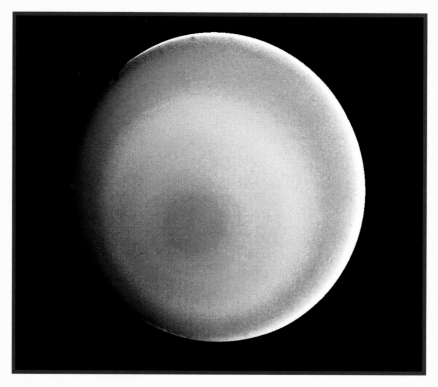

The Hubble Space Telescope has photographed clouds in Uranus's atmosphere.

sphere of Uranus. Hubble is a telescope that orbits around Earth in space. It can take clearer pictures than any telescope on the ground. In 1998, Hubble saw at least 20 bright clouds in the atmosphere of Uranus. They were the brightest clouds seen anywhere in the outer parts of the solar system. These clouds may be made of icy methane crystals. The crystals may have formed from warmer methane gas that bubbled up from deep down in the atmosphere.

BELTS AND ZONES IN THE CLOUDS

Pictures of Uranus show that there are belts and zones in Uranus's clouds. Belts and zones look like stripes going around the planet. The stripes are light-colored and are called zones. The dark-colored stripes are belts. Jupiter is another planet that has belts and zones. Jupiter's belts and zones are easier to see. The belts and zones on Uranus are often blocked out by the smog that covers the planet.

Winds in the belts and zones on Uranus blow in opposite directions. They blow east in a belt and west in a zone. Can you imagine what it would be like to fly a plane across the belts and zones? First, a wind blowing at about 450 miles (720 km) per hour would hit one side of the plane as you passed through a belt. Then a wind blowing just as hard would hit the other side as you passed through a zone. Better keep your seat belt fastened. It would be a bumpy ride!

CHAPTER THREE

What Uranus Is Made Of

Uranus is a type of planet called a gas giant. The other gas giants in our solar system are Jupiter, Saturn, and Neptune. Uranus, like the other gas giants, does not have a solid surface. You could not walk on Uranus the way you can walk on the solid rocks and soil of Earth.

Uranus is made mostly of methane ice and rock. Clouds of methane ice crystals are thinner high in the atmosphere but get thicker down toward the center of the planet. More and more ice crystals press together. They form a sort of slush. Deeper inside Uranus, the slush gets packed even more to form solid ice. Uranus might have a solid center, or core, made of rock. The rocky core could be as large as Earth.

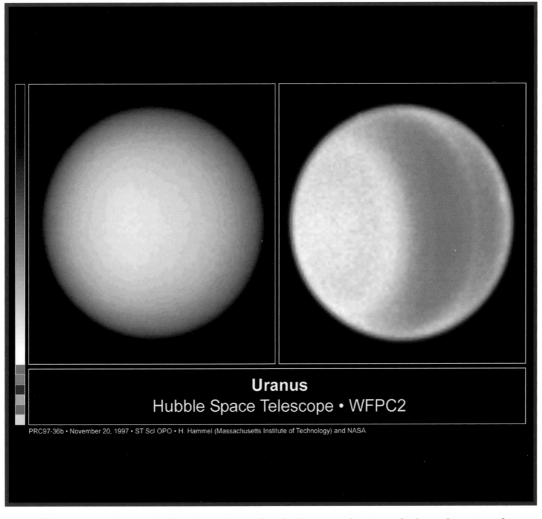

Uranus
Hubble Space Telescope • WFPC2

PRC97-36b • November 20, 1997 • ST ScI OPO • H. Hammel (Massachusetts Institute of Technology) and NASA

Uranus is made mostly of methane ice and rock. Its atmosphere is a thick combination of hydrogen, helium, ethane, and methane. Methane makes the planet appear blue.

The deeper you go inside Uranus, the warmer it gets. The

temperature inside Uranus heats the ice. The warmed ice moves

the way boiling water moves in a pot. The moving ice brings heat from the center of Uranus up to the atmosphere. This makes some parts of the atmosphere warmer than others. Different temperatures in the atmosphere make the wind blow.

Something inside Uranus has turned the planet into a magnet. Astronomers have found a magnetic field around the planet. A

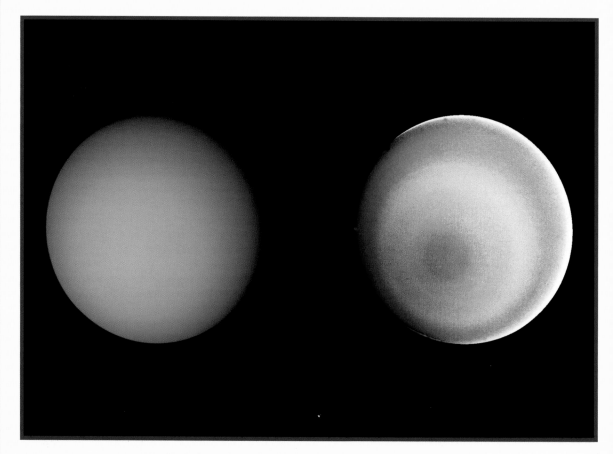

The differing temperatures on Uranus cause winds to blow in the bands and zones of the planet, as shown here.

Many mysteries remain about Uranus that scientists are still trying to figure out. One such mystery involves the planet's core—and what makes it so magnetic.

magnetic field is where the "pull" of a magnet can be detected.

Many of the other planets also have magnetic fields. Sometimes

a planet is turned into a magnet because its core is made of iron.

That is why Earth has a magnetic field. But scientists are not sure

exactly what creates the magnetic field of Uranus.

ICE FROM GAS?

Ice on Uranus is not the kind of ice you make in your freezer. The ice we use on Earth is made from water. Water on Earth is usually a liquid. But ice on Uranus is made from methane. Methane on Earth is usually a colorless, odorless gas. Understanding how water behaves on Earth can help us understand how ice behaves on Uranus.

Water can be a liquid, a solid, or a gas. Very cold, frozen water is solid ice. When it gets warmer, it can melt to become liquid water. If liquid water gets even warmer, it boils. Have you ever watched steam rise off a pot of boiling water? The steam is a gas called water vapor. When steam cools, it becomes water again, and the water can freeze to become ice. The same thing can happen with methane. If the gas methane cools, it becomes a liquid. If it gets even colder, it turns into methane ice.

CHAPTER FOUR

A Planet on Its Side

Uranus moves in a strange way. All the other planets except

Pluto spin as they go around the Sun, but Uranus rolls. Every

planet turns around on its axis. An axis is an imaginary stick going

from the very top to the very bottom of a planet. It is like a pencil

pushed through the center of a ball of clay. The top of the axis is

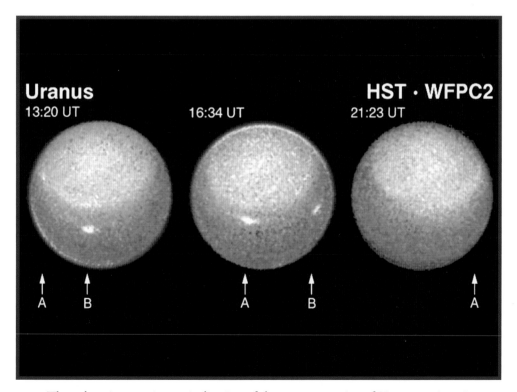

These three images give an indication of the strange rotation of Uranus on its axis.

the north pole of the planet, and the bottom is its south pole.

Most planets have an axis that is slightly tipped. It does not go straight up and down. But the axis of Uranus lies almost flat on its side. So it looks like Uranus is rolling on its axis instead of spinning as it goes around the Sun!

The axis of Uranus gives the planet some very strange seasons. The tilt of a planet on its axis is what makes seasons. Earth is tilted on its

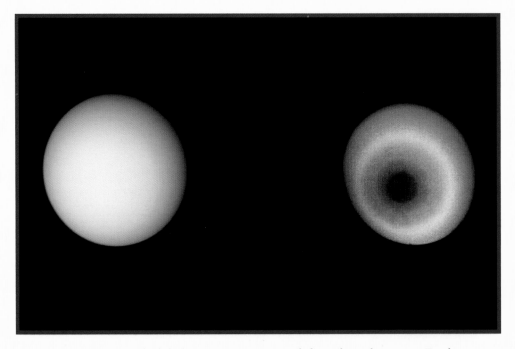

The image on the left shows Uranus as viewed through a telescope on Earth.
The image on the right shows smog over one of Uranus's oddly located poles.

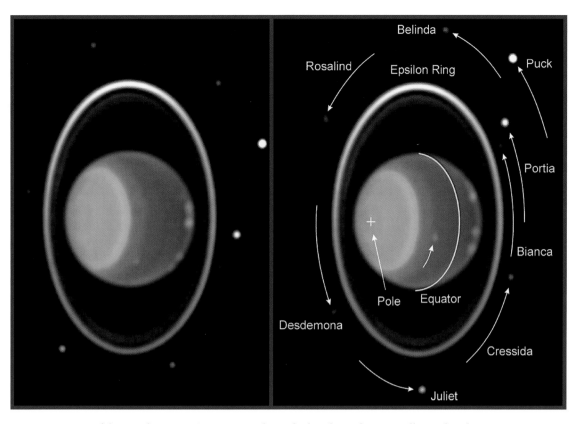

Unlike Earth, Uranus's axis runs through the planet horizontally, so the planet almost seems to be rolling through the universe rather than spinning.

axis so that for half of the year the northern part of Earth gets more heat from the Sun. The other half of the year, the southern part of Earth gets more heat. When it is summer in the north, it is winter in the south. Spring and fall are the seasons in between. Earth's equator, the imaginary line going around the middle of the planet, gets about the same amount of heat from the Sun all year long.

Because of the unusual position of Uranus's axis, its seasons are much longer than those on Earth. While the north pole faces the Sun for half the planet's orbit, the south pole is thrown into complete darkness for that same half year—a period of time equal to 42 Earth-years!

On Uranus, either the north or south pole directly faces the Sun.

It takes Uranus about 84 Earth-years to go around the Sun. So each of

Uranus's four seasons is more than 20 years long!

CHAPTER FIVE

THE RINGS AND MOONS OF URANUS

Uranus, like Jupiter and Saturn, has a set of rings around it. Astronomers looking through telescopes on Earth discovered some of the rings. *Voyager 2* discovered more. There are 11 known rings. All of them circle Uranus above the planet's equator. The rings look dark. They may be made of dust and chunks of ice.

Uranus also has many moons. As of 2003, astronomers had discovered 21 moons orbiting Uranus. Scientists divide these moons into three groups—small moons, icy moons, and newly discovered moons.

The 10 small moons are named Cordelia, Ophelia, Bianca, Cressida, Desdemona, Juliet, Portia, Rosalind, Belinda, and Puck. An average small moon is about the size of a large city on Earth. A

Uranus's strong magnetic field creates rings of particles that encircle the planet, in the same way that rings form around the other gas giants.

moon that size and more than a billion miles away is difficult to

see. The only pictures we have of these moons are very fuzzy.

Scientists do not know much about them, but they think these

small moons are made of ice.

MOONS THAT ACT LIKE SHEEPDOGS

Cordelia and Ophelia, the smallest of the small moons around Uranus, have a special job. They are "shepherding moons." They act like sheepdogs. A sheepdog runs around the outside of a herd of sheep. The dog helps keep the sheep together. The dog will not let sheep stray away from the herd.

Cordelia and Ophelia help keep one of Uranus's rings together. They keep the dust and ice particles of the ring Epsilon in place. Epsilon is the ring that is farthest from Uranus. Cordelia orbits inside the ring, and Ophelia orbits outside. Sheepdogs bark to keep the sheep in line. Cordelia and Ophelia use the force of gravity. Gravity is what pulls one object toward another.

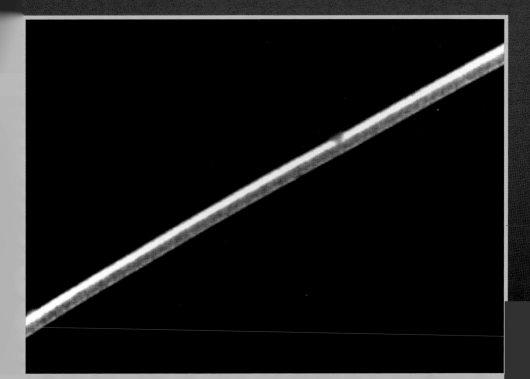

The icy moons are named Miranda, Ariel, Umbriel, Titania, Oberon, Caliban, and Sycorax. The icy moons are larger than the small moons. William Herschel discovered the largest icy moons, Titania and Oberon, in 1787. Titania has a diameter of 1,000 miles (1,610 km). *Voyager 2* found that there is ice and snow on the surfaces of the icy moons. Some icy moons have big holes called craters on their surfaces. Some have grooves. **Meteorites** may have created the craters. Heated ice flowing to the surface may have caused the grooves. Scientists do not know what is inside these moons.

The newly discovered moons are named Prospero, Setebos, Stephano, and 1986 U 10. Scientists first saw them in 1999. These moons are small and orbit as high as 15.5 million miles (24.9 million km) above Uranus. Scientists know nothing about these moons. They still want to study 1986 U 10 because it may not be a moon at all.

A MOON CALLED MIRANDA

The icy moon Miranda has a weird surface. There is nothing else quite like it in our solar system. There are three areas shaped like oval racetracks on Miranda. Astronomers call them ovoids. Ridges and canyons surround the edges of these ovoids. In the center of the ovoids, a jumble of ridges and canyons crisscross each other. Some of the ridges are cliff-like and rise about 12 miles (20 km) from the surface. Miranda also has craters that may have been made by meteorites.

Miranda is only 300 miles (480 km) in diameter. That's almost the distance from Los Angeles to San Francisco. Why does such a small moon have such a strange surface? Miranda has astronomers stumped. It is a moon with a mysterious past.

CHAPTER SIX

HOW URANUS MAY HAVE FORMED

Astronomers think Uranus and the other planets formed from a

swirling cloud of dust and gas about 4.6 billion years ago. The center

of the cloud became the Sun. Then the cloud flattened into a disk. The

dust in the disk had rocks, metal, and ice in it. The gas giant planets

formed in parts of the disk far away from the Sun, where it was cooler.

The rocks and ice came together to form clumps. Then the clumps

Before our solar system formed it was simply a bunch
of smaller particles floating through space.

attracted gas and grew larger. The biggest gas giants, Jupiter and Saturn, formed in parts of the cloud that had the most gas. There was not as much gas left for Uranus. That is why Uranus is smaller than Jupiter or Saturn.

Scientists believe that a huge object, perhaps a meteorite like this one, may have hit Uranus early on, giving it its unique rotation.

Something happened to Uranus after it formed. Astronomers think that an object crashed into the planet. The object may have been as big as Earth. Maybe that is why Uranus spins on its side as it goes around the Sun.

Astronomers have many questions about Uranus. They hope that one day they can send more spacecraft with cameras to Uranus. Maybe these spacecraft will help them answer their questions about this gas giant and how it came to be.

Glossary

astronomers (uh-STRAW-nuh-merz) Astronomers are scientists who study space and the stars and planets.

comet (KOM-it) A comet is a bright object, followed by a tail of dust and ice, that orbits the Sun in a long, oval-shaped path.

meteorites (MEE-tee-uh-rites) Meteorites are rocky, metallic objects from space that hit the surface of a planet or moon.

telescopes (TEL-uh-skopes) Telescopes are instruments used to study things that are far away, such as stars and planets, by making them seem larger and closer.

Did You Know?

▶ A year on Uranus is a long time. A year on a planet is measured by how long it takes the planet to go around the Sun once. One year on Earth is 365 days. A year on Uranus is 30,685 Earth-days, or more than 84 Earth-years.

▶ All but one of the 21 moons of Uranus are named for characters from the works of two English writers—William Shakespeare and Alexander Pope. The moon with the odd name is 1986 U 10. It will be named when scientists decide that it is definitely a moon.

▶ There is little chance that Uranus has any form of life. Uranus is made of poisonous chemicals. It also may be too cold for life to exist. Some types of bacteria or other organisms might be able to survive, but scientists don't know for sure.

▶ The inside and outside of Uranus turn on its axis at different speeds. Parts of the atmosphere make a complete turn in as little as 14 hours. The inner parts turn once every 17 hours and 14 minutes.

Fast Facts

Diameter: 31,765 miles (51,118 km)

Atmosphere: hydrogen, helium, methane, ethane

Time to orbit the Sun (one Uranus-year): 84 Earth-years

Time to turn on axis (one Uranus-day): about 17 Earth-hours

Shortest distance from the Sun: 1.7 billion miles (2.7 billion km)

Greatest distance from the Sun: 1.9 billion miles (3 billion km)

Shortest distance from Earth: 1.6 billion miles (2.6 km)

Greatest distance from Earth: 1.96 billion miles (3.2 billion km)

Temperature range: About –330° F (–200° C) in the upper atmosphere

Surface gravity: 0.90 that of Earth. A person weighing 80 pounds (36 kg) on Earth would weigh about 72 pounds (33 kg) on Uranus.

Number of known moons: 21

Number of known rings: 11

How to Learn More about Uranus

At the Library

Asimov, Isaac, and Richard Hantula. *Uranus.* Milwaukee: Gareth Stevens, 2002.

George, Linda. *Uranus.* San Diego: Kidhaven Press, 2003.

Goss, Tim. *Uranus, Neptune, and Pluto.* Chicago: Heinemann Library, 2003.

Stewart, Melissa. *Uranus.* Danbury, Conn.: Franklin Watts, 2002.

Tocci, Salvatore. *A Look at Uranus.* Danbury, Conn.: Franklin Watts, 2003.

On the Web

Visit our home page for lots of links about Uranus:
http://www.childsworld.com/links.html
Note to Parents, Teachers, and Librarians: We routinely verify our Web links to
make sure they're safe, active sites—so encourage your readers to check them out!

Through the Mail or by Phone

ADLER PLANETARIUM AND ASTRONOMY MUSEUM
1300 South Lake Shore Drive
Chicago, IL 60605-2403
312/922-STAR

NATIONAL AIR AND SPACE MUSEUM
7th and Independence Avenue, S.W.
Washington, DC 20560
202/357-2700

ROSE CENTER FOR EARTH AND SPACE
AMERICAN MUSEUM OF NATURAL HISTORY
Central Park West at 79th Street
New York, NY 10024-5192
212/769-5100

The Sun
Mercury
Venus
Earth
Mars
Jupiter
Saturn
Uranus
Neptune
Pluto

The solar system

Index

About the Author

Darlene R. Stille is a science writer. She has lived in Chicago, Illinois, all her life. When she was in high school, she fell in love with science. While attending the University of Illinois she discovered that she also loved writing. She was fortunate to find a career that allowed her to combine both her interests. Darlene Stille has written about 60 books for young people.